Children in our World

POVERTY AND HUNGER

Louise Spilsbury
Hanane Kai

BARRON'S

First edition for the United States and Canada published in 2017 by Barron's Educational Series, Inc.

First published in Great Britain in 2017 by Wayland

Wayland is an imprint of Hachette Children's Books, part of Hodder & Stoughton.
A Hachette U.K. company.
www.hachette.co.uk
www.hachettechildrens.co.uk

Text © Hodder & Stoughton, 2017
Written by Louise Spilsbury
Illustrations © Hanane Kai, 2017

Edited by Corinne Lucas
Designed by Sophie Wilkins

All inquiries should be addressed to:
Barron's Educational Series, Inc.
250 Wireless Boulevard
Hauppauge, NY 11788
www.barronseduc.com

Library of Congress Control No.: 2017935862

ISBN: 978-1-4380-5019-5

Date of Manufacture: May 2017
Manufactured by: WKT Co. Ltd., Shenzhen, China

Printed in China
9 8 7 6 5 4 3 2 1

The website addresses (URLs) included in this book were valid at the time of going to press. However, it is possible that contents or addresses may have changed since the publication of this book. No responsibility for any such changes can be accepted by either the author or the Publisher.

Contents

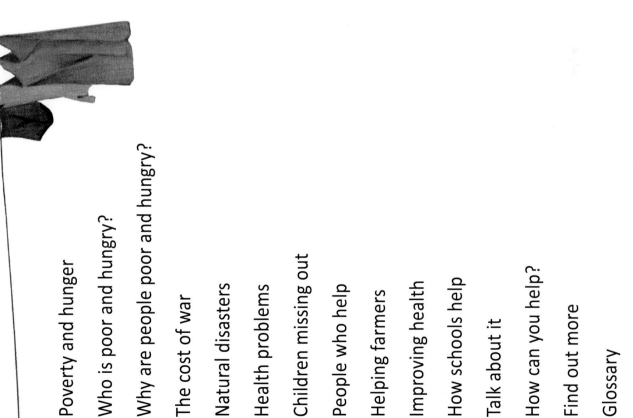

Poverty and hunger

Most people have enough money to buy the things they need, such as food to be healthy, and to buy the items they want, such as treats.

Poverty means a person has little or no money or is very poor. Poor people go hungry day after day because they cannot buy enough food to eat. That kind of hunger makes people weak, tired, and sick. About one in nine people on Earth do not have enough food to lead a healthy and active life.

Who is poor and hungry?

The world's poorest families live in developing countries. In these countries, most people have very little money. Many people have less than $2 a day to buy the food, clean water, clothing, medicine, and shelter they need.

There are poor and hungry people in other countries, too. Poverty and hunger are caused by many things, which are often outside of people's control.

Why are people poor and hungry?

Three-quarters of all hungry people rely on farming for their food. The problem is that they may not have enough money to buy land, tools, or seeds to grow food. If there is no rain, crops and farm animals might die. Without food to eat, people may starve.

Sometimes people are poor because the businesses they worked for closed, or they get very low pay for the jobs they do. Some people have disabilities that prevent them from working. Also, if the person who makes money for a family leaves, the rest of the family may go hungry.

The cost of war

Wars can make people poor and hungry. During a war some people have to fight and cannot work to earn money. Farms may be destroyed and farm animals killed. Bombs are sometimes put in fields, which can prevent farmers from working on the land for years.

People sometimes have to leave their homes because of war. Refugees are people who escape to a new place where they hope to be safe. But, they have no home or job in the new place. That means they cannot earn money to buy food or shelter.

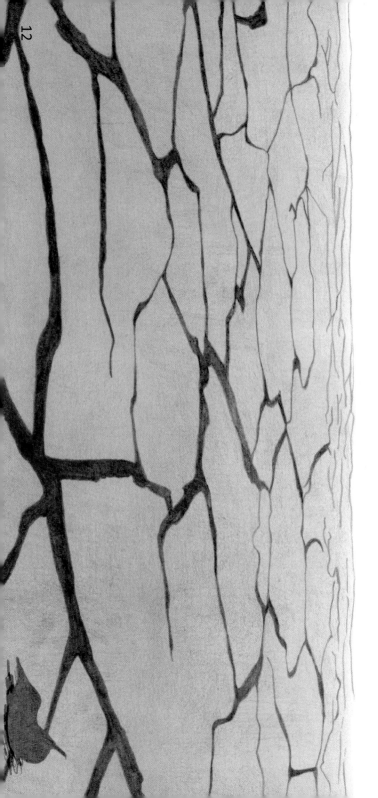

Natural disasters

Natural disasters also cause poverty and hunger, and they can happen anywhere. When a flood covers a field with water, it destroys the crops so the farmer cannot grow food. Hurricanes destroy houses and stores, leaving people without homes, jobs, or food.

The world is getting warmer. Global warming is causing more droughts and other natural disasters. When crops are ruined, there is less food to go around. Then, the price of food goes up. This means more people around the world go hungry.

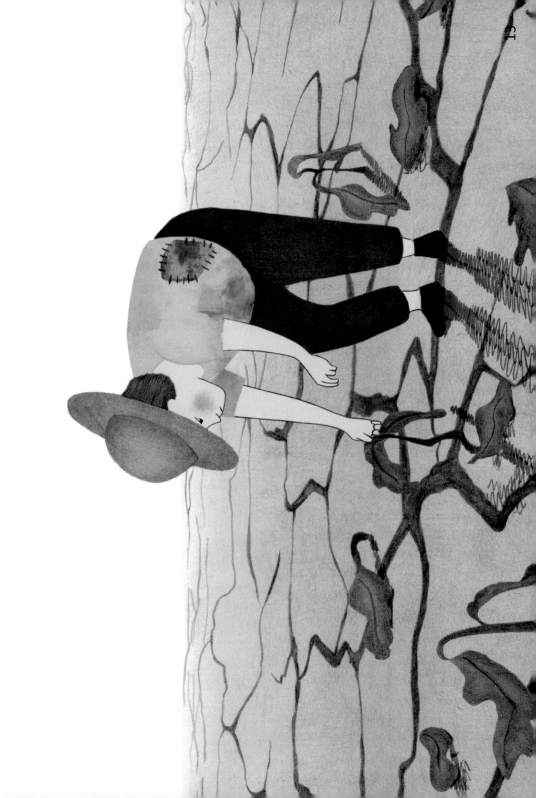

Health problems

Most people have enough money to pay for a warm, safe home to live in. They have clean water to drink and to wash and cook with. They can afford to buy medicine and pay doctors to help them if they get sick.

Poor people may live in damp or cold houses, or they may have no home at all and sleep on the streets instead. Without homes, food, or clean water, people may get sick. When they are sick, they may not be able to afford doctors or medicine to help them.

Children missing out

Poverty is hard on all children. Some may have to miss out on things such as new clothes and school trips. They may be bullied or teased at school. Can you imagine how this feels? Children do not want to be treated differently just because they are poor.

Some families are too poor to buy the uniforms or books children need to go to school. And, some children are too hungry or weak to learn. This makes it hard for them to get a job when they grow up, so their children may also be poor and hungry.

People who help

A charity is a group that helps families and children in need. In some places, charity workers run food banks. People donate cans and boxes of food so poor people can get food from the food banks when they have nothing to eat.

Charities help people change their lives. In developing countries, they give tools to builders or boats to fishing villages so people can work. They help people start businesses. Charities also tell people about poverty so they can raise money to help people in need.

Helping farmers

Charities also help farmers by lending them money to buy tools, machines, and seeds for crops. They show farmers how to use fertilizers to make crops grow bigger and better.

When farmers grow lots of healthy crops, there is more food to eat or sell. This means the farmer's family has more money. They can spend it on school books, clothes, medicine, and other useful things.

Improving health

We all need clean water to be healthy. In developing countries, charities help people build wells and pumps so they can get clean water. They also help people build more sinks and toilets. This helps people avoid diseases.

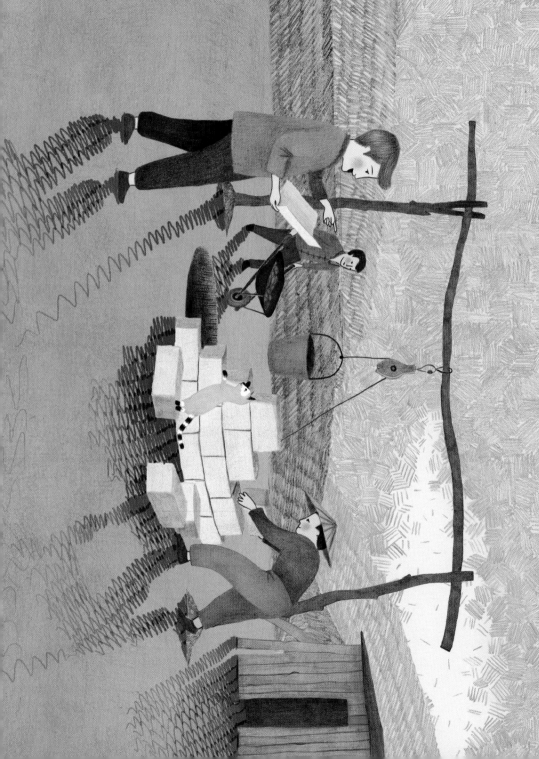

Charities also help people build hospitals. They teach nurses and doctors, and they provide medicine. They make sure babies get the health checks they need. When children grow up healthy, they have a better chance of staying healthy as adults.

How schools help

It is hard to learn if you are hungry. Imagine going to school with an empty stomach. Hunger makes it difficult to pay attention in class and to remember things. Schools can provide free lunches so children do not go hungry.

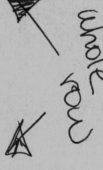

People help children in developing countries by building schools and training teachers. This means more children get the chance to learn. When children get an education, it is easier for them to get a better paid job and escape up.

Talk about it

It is normal to feel sad or angry that some people live in poverty and hunger when other people have so much. If you are upset, talk to an adult about how you feel. He or she can help you.

Things are getting better all the time. There are fewer poor and hungry people today than there were 20 years ago. That is because people have done things to make a difference, and they are still helping today.

How can you help?

It feels good to help people. There are lots of things you could do. You could give old toys, books, clothes, or other items to a thrift store. You could ask your family to give cans of food to a food bank. You could bake cakes to raise money for a charity that helps people who are poor and hungry around the world. What ideas do you have?

Find out more

Books

Beatrice's Goat
Page McBrier, Aladdin Paperbacks, 2004

Maddi's Fridge
Lois Brandt, Flashlight Press, 2014

Crenshaw
Katherine Applegate, Feiwel & Friends, 2015

Websites

Save the Children works to protect children in need all over the world.
www.savethechildren.org

The Red Cross is a charity that helps victims of war and natural disasters.
www.redcross.org

UNICEF Kid Power is a charity that gives kids the chance to help save lives.
www.unicefkidpower.org

Feeding America provides food to people in need through a system of food banks across the country.
www.feedingamerica.org

Food Banks Canada helps people living with hunger by supporting food banks and food agencies in communities throughout Canada.
www.foodbankscanada.ca

Glossary

charity a group that helps people in need

crops plants grown for food

developing countries places around the world where people rely mostly on farming for food, earn very little money, do not always go to school, and have little or no health care

disability a condition that limits what someone can do, such as not being able to see or having trouble learning

disease another word for *illness or sickness*

drought when a place gets little or no rain for months or years

fertilizer a substance that helps plants grow bigger and better

flood when water overflows onto land and through fields, streets, and houses causing damage

food bank a place people in need can go to receive food for free

global warming a rise in Earth's temperature

hurricane a dangerous storm with powerful winds

natural disasters natural events that cause great damage, such as hurricanes, floods, and earthquakes

refugee a person who leaves his or her home country to find a safer place to live

starve to suffer or to die from hunger

Index